DEDICATION

To my wonderful Son, Stephen and
my very talented Daughter, Cheryl,
for giving me so much happiness and love,
making my life complete.

Copyright © 2020 Gladeta Winter
All rights reserved.
ISBN: 9798553364144

Contents

ACKNOWLEDGMENTS

Illustrations with thanks to my Daughter, Cheryl.

A New Challenge

Sitting by the fireside all cosy and warm
My thoughts began to wander down memory lane
So much has happened down life's rocky road
Where over the years I used poetry to explain

As I sat there reminiscing, I glanced out of a window
To be greeted with such a very charming sight
As a large flurry of snowflakes was gently falling
Gradually covering everywhere in glittering white

This very tranquil scene just took my breath away
And was such a good omen for a New Challenge to begin
To get some of my poems printed for safekeeping
With the help of a clever daughter who is my kith and kin…

Spring

Bluebells

Whilst strolling through a woodland glade

Enjoying my walk in the cool dapple shade
I suddenly stopped as I became aware
Of a mass of blue in front of me there

I stood transfixed by such a wonderous sight
There were millions of bluebells I saw outright
Their sweet scented perfume filled the air
Such a beautiful view was beyond compare

How long I stood there I could not tell
For I just could not leave that woodland dell
So soft was the breeze as it wafted through
Like a gentle wave in that sea of blue

With gladdened eye and heart on sleeve
I finally had to take my leave
Of that wonderful sight in the woodland glade
Such beauty so fragile that soon it would fade

Now as I look through my window pane
Watching the rain pouring down again
My thoughts return to that woodland dell
Where I found such peace with the wild bluebell

Spring Concert

Those cold dark days of winter

Have now finally gone at last

And the lovely Springtime season

Has arrived to help us all adjust

There are so many early spring flowers

Popping up from their winter rest

As well as masses of golden daffodils

Blossoming at their very best

We can take a stroll in parks and woods

And see new life beginning there

With hedges and trees all showing off

Their fresh green mantle everywhere

When you find those breath-taking views

It can never fail to impress

Seeing Mother Nature in all her glory

As the warmer days progress

Now Easter is almost upon us

Which is such a pretty festive time

With lots of traditions and treats for us all

To enjoy in the warm Spring sunshine

Delicious hot cross buns and chocolate eggs
Are available for a very special treat
And social gatherings arranged outdoors
For everyone to come and meet

So welcome to our sing-a-long Spring concert
Which is being held this afternoon
Our Leader has chosen some familiar songs to sing
And we will do our very best to stay in tune

In addition, there is also being organised
An Easter Bonnet competition
For anyone who would like to enter
Depending on their artistic inspiration

The bonnets will all be carefully judged
Until one is chosen from the rest
To win a prize will be quite exciting
As we find out which bonnet is the best

This means that our Spring Concert
Will be slightly different just for today
But hopefully it will give us lots of fun
And much enjoyment in every way

Sometimes life can be very hard
So having some unexpected surprises
Can help to find much needed happiness
Whenever the situation arises

So this afternoon try to leave all your worries
Behind you for a little while
As you sing a along with us and join in
All the laughter with a great big smile

Now we invite you all to sit back and relax
As we do our very best to entertain you
With our Leader's musical expertise guiding us
As we enjoy our Spring Concert all through

Springtime

Now the cold days of Winter are on the wane
And Springtime is slowly coming back again
As delicate little snowdrops can be found
Pushing their little white heads up through the ground

As the days grow longer and a little warmer
New life begins wherever you may wander
A walk through a woodland park is very exhilarating
Seeing all the changes that Spring is now creating

Springtime is such a pretty season to enjoy in so many ways
With delightful flowers and bird song making lots of joyful days
Time passes by so quickly as there is so much to behold
With Nature's splendid new beginning after all the Winter's cold

A Proud Mum

Another year has flown away

And once again it is your Birthday

Hope you will celebrate in style

With lots of fun and a great big smile

Thanks for all you do for me when I am in a whirl

You are my very precious lovely little girl

I am a very proud Mum of all you have done

With all the accolades and medals you have Won

You are so clever, helpful and kind

Always giving me such peace of mind

All the best for your Special Day

May you have joy and happiness all the way

From Old Dad and Me

You are as pretty as a picture
And as busy as a bee
You are such a very special daughter
Who means the world to your old Dad and me

Always helping us in every way
Showing us how things should be
Such a very caring daughter
Who looks after your old Dad and me

So my lovely darling daughter
It is very plain to see
We both love you so very much
And wish you all the best from your old Dad and me

Congratulations

You took up the challenge for a very good cause
Entering the Portsmouth 10 mile Marathon Run
And you succeeded in crossing the finishing line
After some very hard work and a whole lot of fun

The weather turned out to be so extremely wet
So making it all the more difficult and tough
But you managed to keep going around the course
To finally win through all that rain so rough

It was such a truly great effort for you to achieve
And we are so impressed and very proud of you
Many Congratulations and a Big Well Done
You certainly deserve your Special Medal too

A Dear Mum

Although the days slip by so swiftly
Many wonderful memories stay in mind
As somewhere there is a beautiful place
That all our lost dear loved ones can find

So when you see a lovely rose garden
Or hear birds sing on a bright sunny day
All these beautiful things will remind you
That your dear Mum is never very far away

Try to keep thinking of all the good times
That you shared with your dear Mum
To help you find peace and solace
In the many hard years to come

And as this very sad day returns once again
You know we shall all be thinking of you
Hoping you will find consolation together
In memory of your dear Mum so good and true

Half Marathon Success

Now that you have succeeded once again
By completing your 2nd Marathon Run
It's many "Congrats" from us to you
We are so proud of all you have done

You are such a very caring clever girl
Giving so much effort for this Special Event
And certainly deserve your well earned Medal
To commemorate your very find achievement

Daughter's Birthday

From the day you were born
On that Saturday morn
On a special day in March
You were loved from the heart
Right from the start
Our new baby girl was just great

The years have just flown
And you have now grown
Into such a kind and clever daughter
Of whom we are so proud
And sing your praises out loud
As we know you will never alter

May you have much pleasure
With gifts you can treasure
As celebrations get under way
We send you all our best wishes
With lots of love and kisses
For your very Special Birthday

A Special Daughter

You are a very Special Daughter
So clever and so kind
Always there to help me
With things I can't do or find

You make my life so very happy
And quite content in every way
I couldn't be more proud of you
Counting my blessings every day

So here's wishing you a Happy Birthday
And lots of happiness too
Do hope you have a jolly good time
With some exciting surprises just for you

Easter Reflections

Easter comes around again
Heralding the Spring
As we see so many golden daffodils
And hear all the little birds sing

It is such a very pretty time
When everything starts anew
Little lambs frisking in the fields
And warm sunshine in skies of blue

There are hot cross buns a plenty
To commemorate this religious time
Then lovely Easter eggs to celebrate
Made of delicious chocolate so fine

We always had such a lot of fun
When you were with us dear
But now there is an empty place
That brings much sadness and a tear

But happy fond memories will never fade
As every Eastertime brings much pleasure
And all those many joyful times now gone by
Will always be there in our thoughts to treasure

Our New Choir

It all started at the beginning of the year
When Churchill/Millstream supported a New Choir
And asked our friend to set it all up for us
On Wednesdays each week for an hour

At first it went well but there was a small hitch
As Wednesdays clashed with other events
So it was changed to Mondays which helped a lot
And everyone could relax as it made more sense

We thoroughly enjoy our weekly hour
And welcome all from other lodges to try
As the music and songs are so well known
Singing together lifts the spirits way up high

Gradually our harmonising has steadily improved
And we have even given a small concert or two
With our friend and her husband showing the way
Our New Choir has certainly come through

To our surprise our fame is spreading
Being recently included in the National press
We were all so amazed and thrilled to see
Our story and photo shown in the Daily Mail & Express

And now we have made a CD for Christmas
Which has turned out to be a hit with us all
With lyrics and music by our talented friend
All proceeds will go to a charity on call

So a great big thank you to our friends
For all the very hard work that they do
In making our New Choir so very enjoyable
And giving us such pleasure and a lot of fun too

Songs from the "Shows"

Welcome to our first Concert of the year
Full of popular songs from the shows
Bringing back some happy memories
Of all those favourites everyone knows

There are so many delightful songs to sing
It is no wonder we are spoilt for choice
But our leader has selected some popular tunes
That should suit every type of voice

We do hope you will all join in
With those melodies you love to hear
And enjoy an evening of splendid music
Singing popular songs loud and clear

Our 2017 year ended with some success
When we made a Christmas film and CD
And were so delighted with the proceeds
All collected for the Churchill Cancer charity

This will be our third consecutive year
And our Choir is gradually making progress
With some very welcome new members
To help maintain our general status

Monday mornings are still such a treat
Along with our leader and her husband, whom we admire
With her brilliant training and dedication
And all his amazing anecdotes that inspire

Spring is such a lovely time of year
After all those cold, dark winter days
So our leader has very cleverly put together
This Concert to give some cheer in many ways

Easter has just past with all the celebrations
Hot cross buns and chocolate eggs galore
And there are masses of golden daffodils to see
Heralding warmer times to enjoy once more

So much to look forward to from now on
It is sometimes good to stop a while and ponder
As the pretty springtime turns into beautiful summer
We realise this country of ours is full of wonder

Thank you all for coming this evening
It gives us much pleasure to entertain you
Hope the musical program gives you some joy
With those "Songs from the Shows" you all knew

Sad News

So sorry to hear your bad news my dear
It must be such a worrying time for you
But then always being such a tough fighter
Your strength and courage will see you through

We have shared many years of friendship
Keeping in touch as much as we could
Enjoying some very good times together
And swapping our memories bad and good

You know we all wish you the best of luck
Do hope everything goes according to plan
So you can once again return to normal
And carry on living your life as well as you can

Much Loved Mum

Always there to help and guide you
Very loving and such a kind Mum too
Every day always caring so much
Ready to comfort with her soft touch
Your much loved Mum was truly one of the best

Doing all she could with vigour and zest
Enduring all the troubles that came her way
And through all the toil and strife each day
Rendering such tenderness to enthrall
Many wonderful years she was with you all

Until sadly she could no longer be there as before
Your much loved Mum will be remembered forever more

Pen-Pal USA

In an exciting country, far over the sea
I have a super Pen-Pal, who writes to me
We met quite by chance one fine sunny day
Whilst stopping for a meal in Jackson, USA

From that moment on, our friendship began
And over the years, we have kept to our plan
To regularly write about our family news
And of each other's countries, with many views

We have tried several ways to keep in touch
By telephone, tape, photographs and such
Interesting long letters come through the post
And it's these welcome letters I like the most

On special occasions, lovely gifts come through
When my dear Pen-Pal shows her friendship true
Words cannot express what it means to me
To have such a kind, loyal Pen-Pal as Carrielee

Friendship

We have been friends for so many years
It was a friendship so full of joy
Over all that time
We were just fine
Through happy times and some tears

It all started when we were both very young
We first met and our friendship began
Working together every day
It was a good team all the way
And our friendship turned into such fun

As time passed by we went our separate ways
Having to look after our growing families
But we stayed in touch
As it meant so much
To meet up and share more enjoyable days

Now as I look back on those happy times
I know my dear friend wanted it said
That we both had a ball
And we so enjoyed it all
As our true friendship fulfilled all the signs

Fate

Sometimes I sit and wonder
What life is all about
When so much grief surrounds us
As fate deals such a clout

Sometimes it seems that nothing
Can ever stem the pain
Of losing a very dear loved one
When fate has struck again

Sometimes there must be an answer
To all this fragile life
But when the tears keep falling
Then fate feels just like a knife

My Dream Come True

My daughter booked a surprise holiday to India
Which was completely out of the blue
To go and see the beautiful Taj Mahal Monument
Something I have always wanted to do

We were both very excited and a bit apprehensive
To be visiting such a remarkable country
But we had the most interesting holiday together
With so many amazing places on our itinerary

To finally see the magnificent Taj Mahal was so impressive
And was such an emotional moment to retain
It just sparkled in the sunlight which took our breath away
A most beautiful sight we will never see again

We also went on an interesting safari tour
Through thick scrub and park land a vast area of ground
And saw a great many wild animals and unusual birds
Including a fully grown tiger just wandering around

We were taken by coach through busy villages and towns
Which made it such a wonderful holiday out of the blue
And it all ended with a shopping spree in a very grand hotel
Spectacularly making my lifetime Dream Come True

Rosie

She came to you as a very tiny chick
All those many years ago
And she grew into the sweetest bird
That all of us could ever know

To hear her song and very loud call
As you entered through the door
Was such a very welcoming sound
That will be in our thoughts ever more

She could perform many clever tricks
That gave so much fun and pleasure
And she had such a long and happy life
With many lovely memories to treasure

Now very sadly your sweet little Rosie
Has reached her journey's end
But she will always be remembered
As your truly Special little feathered friend

Summer

Golden Anniversary

It started as a holiday romance
And blossomed into a love so true
Lasting for many splendid years
Since the day you both said "I do"

It is such a very fine achievement
Being there together for so long
Sharing life's difficult "ups and "downs"
Helping each other with a love so strong

So here's wishing you all the very best
With many Congratulations and Cheers
Hope you both have a really great time
Celebrating your 50 Golden Years

50 Golden Years

You met just by chance all those years ago
And your love for each other just grew
Then you finally Wed on that fine Spring Day
Declaring your Special love, so true

It is such a very splendid achievement
To have stayed together for all that time
Sharing life's many joys and sorrows
Always there for each other, come rain or shine

So here's wishing you all the very best
With many Congratulations and hearty Good Cheers
Hope you both have a really great time
As you celebrate your 50 Golden Years

Somebody cares

Somebody cares a lot for you
Wherever you are, whatever you do

Cares if you are troubled, or ill, or sad
Cares if you are happy, well and glad

Somebody loves your voice, your smile
The touch of your hand that makes life worthwhile

And someday perhaps, as the years roll on
You will look behind o'er the road we've gone

Then you will discover by and by
The someone caring so much was I

Love

Love is like a beautiful garden
That gives much pleasure to us all
And love is like the four seasons
Giving us wonderful changes to recall

Love is like a pretty fountain
That splashes and sparkles in the sun
And love is like a sacred prayer
Which is said when day is done

Love is like a favourite tune
That brings fond memories to mind
And love is like a special poem
With words that help us unwind

Love is like the early sunrise
That heralds another new day
And love is like a glowing sunset
Giving such a spectacular display

Love is always there to guide us
No matter where we go or what we do
And it will stay in our hearts forever
For those lost dear loved ones we once knew

Rusty

We chose you as a puppy

All those many years ago

And you changed our lives completely

Because we loved you so

You gave us joy and friendship

In the only way you knew

And in all those years we shared

Our love for you just grew

Now the time we had together

Has sadly come to an end

We miss you dear old RUSTY

OUR FAITHFUL DOGGY FRIEND

Special Day

It's that time again – your Birthday is here
And we do hope you have a good time dear
With plenty of presents and surprises too
All making it a very Special Day for you

It just seems like it was only yesterday
When there safely in our arms you lay
Such a lovely baby so precious and small
Giving so much happiness and joy to us all

Now you have grown up through the years
Sharing lots of happiness and a few tears
But always showing us how much you care
Such love and devotion is so very rare

We do hope it all goes with a swing
And you enjoy yourself with everything
Have a great celebration - as we both say
All the best, darling, for a Happy Birthday

50th Birthday Milestone

Many congratulations and best wishes
On reaching your 50th year
A very iconic milestone to celebrate
After all you have achieved my dear

A wonderful Thailand holiday is planned
To mark such a Special occasion
Where you can play golf and relax by the pool
In a nice warm climate in that lovely location

You have grown into a very kind caring girl
Since that lovely day you were born
On a Saturday in March
A very sunny Easter morn

So clever with all your talent and expertise
Using computers and technology on line
It is so impressive on what you can do
As well as all your organising skills so fine

You have certainly had your "ups" and "downs"
Throughout all the years it's true
Some very good times and some quite sad
But you always manage to come through

So here's wishing you every success
In all the years there are to come
You have become such a lovely daughter
Making me the world's most proudest Mum

Our Holiday

We packed our bags and off we went
To stay by the coast for a nice rest
We planned to see some lovely views
Something we all like doing the best

Plenty of interesting things to do
As we toured around the bays
Sunshine and blue skies wherever we went
And great spectacular, sparkling waves

Beautiful beaches with golden sands
Rocks and seaweed scattered on shore
A large collection of bright coloured shells
To collect for a memento of what we saw

The hotel was very near the sea
Our room was nice and clean
The food they served was quite superb
And views from our room the best ever seen

Finally our holiday had come to an end
And it was time to say "Good-bye"
We had all enjoyed our few days of rest
Now it was back home with a great big sigh!

Special Cousin's 80th Year

Well done on reaching such a Special milestone
It is a remarkable achievement in this day and age
You have had to face so much throughout the years
But now you can be proud as you begin another page

Sincerely hope you have a really wonderful day
Celebrating your tremendous long life span
And no doubt all your loving family will be there
So you can thoroughly enjoy being with your clan

We send you all our very best wishes, dear Cousin
You certainly deserve a Birthday full of good cheer
May all your precious dreams and hopes be fulfilled
As you savour every moment with those you hold dear

Poignant 52nd Anniversary

So many years have now passed by
Since that lovely day 7th June 1952
But we have managed to stay together
With a love that is forever true

And as we look back over our lives
We remember those wonderful days
When we were such a happy family
Having lots of fun in so many ways

Now we are in our "autumn" years
Somehow we just keep plodding on
Although the sorrow is always there
When we tragically lost our darling Son

But through it all we have done our best
Sharing our lives with lots of joy and tears
And so far we have survived life's rocky road
Do hope we can go on for a few more years

Anniversary Devotion

Another year, another Anniversary
How quickly they slip by
But you are both still there side by side
With a love so strong, you can't go wrong
Such devotion you just can't hide

So many years have come and gone
With ups and downs galore
But you are an inspiration to us all
With hearts so true, from both of you
A super couple whose love will never fall

Many congratulations and best wishes
For this your very Special Day
Celebrating your love so tender and true
With your family there, showing they care
May joy and happiness abound for you

Diamond Anniversary

It is now 60 years since we were Wed
On that lovely day in June
And still our love has kept us together
As time goes passing by all too soon

As we look back over our wedded bliss
There has been plenty of laughter and tears
But we have tried to do our very best
Sharing the good times, hardships and fears

Having two really wonderful children
Made our little family so complete
But now we face such a lot of sadness
That is so very hard for us to defeat

As the loss of our very dearest Son
Was such a terrible emotional strain
And caused us so much heartache
Our lives could never be right again

But through all our darkest hours
Our darling daughter is always there
Giving us such courage and comfort
And helping us celebrate our 60th year

So many congratulations to both of us
Old Glad and Geoff now Darby and Joan
Let us hope we still have a few more years
To celebrate together with a love that's grown

Friend's 60th Anniversary

Many congratulations on reaching 60 years of married life
Such a wonderful achievement for you both to share
You must have many precious memories as man and wife
Which you can look back on with great pride and care

Although we have only known each other for a short time
From when we moved into "Dean Lodge" on the first floor
We have become good neighbours getting along just fine
Having chats whenever we met in the lounge or corridor

Do hope you both have a really marvellous celebration
Together with all your many family and friends
As they all give you their love and deep affection
For your long happy marriage that has surpassed all trends

Edna's - 100th Birthday

We celebrated your 99th Birthday last year
In fine style when you were the Guest of Honour
And serenaded at a beautifully decorated table
By a very handsome talented Waiter/Tenor

Now one year on from that excellent event
You have now amazingly reached your 100th year
Such another great achievement that we all admire
Your longevity and looking so well deserves a big cheer

But in this very strange year we are under a lockdown
And only small gatherings so far are being allowed
Thus we do hope you will be able to enjoy this little party
With your Dean Lodge friends in such a small crowd

You should hopefully receive a Royal card
From Her Majesty, The Queen, whom we admire
To commemorate your excellent 100th year
A very Special keepsake for you to acquire

So all our sincerest congratulations Dear Edna
On reaching such a magnificent milestone with such agility
You certainly deserve every happiness and good health
As you continue to live your long life to the best of your ability

Her Majesty – The Queen

Whilst watching the wildlife on a platform in a tree
Such a very poignant moment that made history
It was tragic news of her father that made her a Queen
What a sudden life changing episode it had all been
For 60 long years she has reigned supreme
A beautiful wife and mother – Her Majesty, the Queen

She rode in great style to her Coronation
And made her pledge in front of the Nation
Looking resplendent in her glittering golden coach
She has carried out her duties beyond reproach
With her loving husband and family there as a team
Such a dedicated and loyal person – Her Majesty, the Queen

Now there are plans for some spectacular celebrations
With a multitude of preparations and organisations
To mark such an astonishingly great achievement to begin
And to make sure that all the pageants and parties fit in
It will be such a very Special Year, with a Royal Theme
An Olympic Diamond Jubilee for – Her Majesty, the Queen

Treasured Friendship

I have treasured our long friendship
From the very first time we met
When we worked together so well
And then our true friendship was set

All those happy meetings we shared
So many good times to recall
Over so many years of friendship
We both really did have a ball

But no matter what life has in store
To have such a loyal friend
Is such a great honour for me
So may our friendship never end

But the sad news you are not well
Is so hard to believe that it is true
And my thoughts and love are there
For my very best friend - that is you

Moving Home

It has been such a most unusual year
Since my dear husband sadly passed away
On 17th September 2013, leaving me alone
So I decided to move, as I just couldn't stay

It was the biggest, hardest decision to make
To sell our family home after so many years
But with my dear daughter's help I managed it all
And left my old life behind, after a few tears

Now I have moved to Southbourne by the sea
Into a very comfortable, cosy little flat
Where I can thoroughly enjoy this pretty area
And my daughter can visit for a "cuppa" and chat

We have also been to India to see the Taj Mahal
Such a surprise holiday right out of the blue
A fantastic place I have always longed to see
So making my lifelong dream come true

It has been quite hectic to get settled down
Such a lot of items to sort out and unpack
But on the whole quite an exciting time
Having to buy many new things that I lack

With my daughter so near makes it all worthwhile
And I am no longer feeling so lonely and lost
As now I can see her more often
Which was the main plan no matter the cost

So many grateful thanks to my dear daughter
For everything that she did and, as I said
I am very pleased to be much closer to her now
And hope there are a few more happy years ahead

A Friend's Move

We have been friends for so many years
A true friendship to treasure
Over all that time
It has just been fine
Through happy times and some tears

Now you have decided to move my dear
To be nearer to your lovely daughter
It was a very good test
And you gave it your best
So at last there is no more loneliness or fear

A nice new home to enjoy from now on
Which was the right choice to make
Now you are all set
For the new life you can get
Welcome to sunny Dorset with cares all gone

Autumn

Honey

You had your dog Honey for so many years
Such a good companion and friend
Giving you so much joy and pleasure
With loved and loyalty right to the end

She had such a good home from the start
With "walkies" and nice "treats" every day
Making her so happy and quite fulfilled
Such a very contented Honey in every way

Now sadly your dog Honey has had to go
And it is hard to say goodbye without a tear
But all those lovely memories will never fade
Of your wonderful "doggy" friend so dear

Some Cheer

This is just another little card
To try to give you some cheer
Such a shock to hear the news is not good
And an operation is needed my dear

Medicine has improved by leaps and bounds
Since those early days of yore
So there is now a great deal more hope
For a full recovery to good health once more

You are so brave and very strong
As you face such a difficult time
Fighting with such courage and resolve
Until finally you are back in your prime

No doubt it will all take a few weeks
To recover after all the treatment is done
And we send you all our very best wishes
Hoping your battle is soon well and truly Won

My Prayer

May your memories be filled with joy
May peace be yours in heaven above
May he keep you safe from all harm
May you be blessed with all His love

May tuneful music come your way
May Ted your little mascot be there
May you find happiness every day
May He keep you safe with His care

In Fond Remembrance

Happy the memories of those years gone by
Precious the moments that we hold so dear
Sunny the days when there was no need to cry
Unforgettable the times when dear ones were near

Gone are the days when you were there
Special was our family having fun together
Joyous were the times we could all share
Deep is our love that will stay forever

A Very Special Mum

She was a very Special Mum
Who gave you so much care
Working hard all her life
And always being there

She was a very Special Mum
Who did all she could for you
No one could ever take her place
Such wonderful people are so few

She was a very Special Mum
Who gave you all her love
And now she rests in quiet peace
In God's perfect Heaven above

Courageous Birthday

Once again your Birthday comes along
And still you go gallantly plodding on
Doing your best to cope as the years go by
With all life's problems that make us cry

You have faced so many tragedies
And had the very worst illness of all
But your courage and determination
Has pulled you through without a fall

Now you can celebrate your Birthday
With your head held high at last
After all you have suffered over the years
It is amazing your very long fight is now in the past

So all our best wishes for a lovely Day
Hope it is a very happy one in every way
With all your loving family there too
Can only make it a perfect Day for you

A Tribute to Mum

Such a very Special Mum with a heart of gold
Always there in good times and bad
Keeping her family safe and warm
No matter what strife or troubles she had

She worked so very hard all her life
Facing the difficult times with a smile
Always so very loving and caring
With such true dedication all the while

It is so hard to lose such a very dear Mum
And each year that sad day brings tears
But all those precious happy memories she gave you
Will stay with you forever during the passing years

Memories

Another year goes passing by
But precious memories will never fade
Of all those wonderful times you shared
And all the love your dear husband gave

Always ready with a helping hand
He was there when times were bad
But his lovely smile and lots of laughter
Would make everybody feel so glad

So as you cope with life's ups and downs
And this sad day returns as before
Remember all those happy days gone by
Treasuring your dear husband's memory ever more

It Doesn't Matter

It doesn't matter where you go
Nor does it matter what you do
The love that you have known
Will always be there for you

It doesn't matter who you are
Nor does it matter why it is so
The love that you have shared
Will always constantly grow

It doesn't matter which way is best
Nor does it matter when you start
The love that you needed so much
Will always be there in your heart

The Love You Had

The love you had is always there
No matter where you may go
The love you knew is everywhere
In all the beautiful flowers that grow

The love you had will never fade
And will stay strong and true
The love you knew will always be
Of the greatest comfort to you

The love you had was so divine
You both shared it from the start
The love you knew will forever be
Kept safe within your heart

Wherever You May Go

Wherever you may go
Whatever you may do
All the love you have shown
Will always be there for you

Whoever you may be
Wherever you may go
All the love you have shared
Will always forever grow

Whichever way may be best
Whenever you may start
All the love you were given
Will always be there in your heart

Sadness

So many tears have fallen
With so much sadness and pain
So many hearts were broken
With no going back again

So many precious memories
With so much fun and joy
So many happy sunny days
With so much love for our boy

An Extraordinary Year

I moved to sunny Dorset
In January of this year
After losing my poor husband
Whom I loved so very dear

My whole life changed completely
Nothing was ever the same
So to be closer to my dear daughter
Became my foremost aim

It was such a hard decision
Selling our home after many years
But with lots of help I managed it
Facing the future with some fears

Now I live in Southbourne by the sea
In a very cosy Churchill flat
Where everyone is so kind and friendly
Getting together for a coffee and chat

It has been quite hectic settling in
With so much to sort out and unpack
But on the whole an exciting time
Buying many new things that I lack

Then a fantastic trip to see the Taj Mahal
My daughter's surprise right out of the blue
Such a magical place I had longed to see
Making my lifelong dream come true

So with all my Churchill friends around
And my lovely daughter so close by
I am no longer feeling lonely or lost
And so glad I gave moving here a try

Birthday Celebrations

Another year has quickly flown away
And once again it is your Birthday
Hope you will celebrate in great style
With lots of fun and a lovely big smile

Thanks for everything you do for me
You are my very precious little "Wheely"
I am so proud of all you have done
And the accolades and medals you have won

You are very clever, helpful and kind
Always giving me such peace of mind
So all the best for your Special Day
May you have joy and happiness all the way

Local Air Festival

Those hazy lazy days of summer
Are now on the wane
And soon those beautiful colours of autumn
Will be coming back again

But before the change of these seasons
The annual Bournemouth Air Festival takes place
To commemorate the RAF achievements
And the many courageous air battles they had to face

This year the Red Arrows Display team
Will not be performing their flying skills
As this year they are based in the USA
Giving Americans the benefit of their many thrills

So we have organised an afternoon Concert
With some popular songs for us all to sing
And we hope we can pass on this wonderful feeling
That such an enjoyable afternoon will bring

Bournemouth Air Show

It was indeed our darkest hour
When "World War II" was declared
A war that would last for six long years
For which we were all so unprepared

Thousands of families were torn apart
When their loved ones were sent to war
But through all the carnage and devastation
They found comradeship not known before

There were many fierce conflicts over land and sea
And tremendous "dog-fights" in the air
Enemy planes dropping their deadly bombs
Destroying everything in sight without a care

It was a tragic horrendous time for everyone
So much hardship, destruction and distress
But through it all our courage held firm
And we all worked together to clear up the mess

This terrible war was very cruel and violent
But our brave troops fought hard and well
Defeating the foe at last but at a very high cost
As many precious lives were taken in that hell

What a great relief when the "All Clear" sounded
And we knew that this horrible war was finally over
With great rejoicing we sang Vera Lynn's famous songs
We'll Meet Again and The White Cliffs of Dover

Now every year we honour those valiant troops
With a "Fly Past" of vintage planes in late summer
Bringing back those familiar sights once again
An impressive Spitfire, Hurricane and Wellington Bomber

So raise your glasses to those lost loved ones
They were such very courageous troops of war
Who gave their all to win back our freedom
And regain peace in our country once more

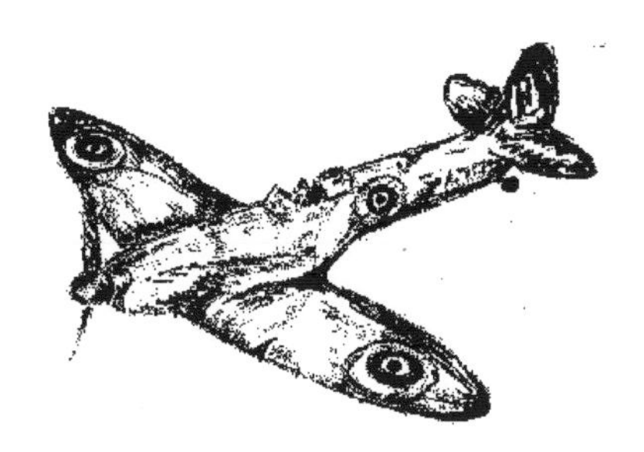

RAF Centenary Festival

Every year at around this time
The Bournemouth Air Festival takes place
With "fly-pasts" of some quite unique planes
And fast modern jets that barely leave a trace

The Festival goes on for three whole days
To commemorate those brave boys in blue
A magnificent showcase of flying expertise
With many familiar airplanes old and new

Now the RAF are celebrating their Centenary year
As it is 100 years since men had the urge to fly
In those very strange aircraft so flimsy and crude
Which took such courage and nerve just to try

Those first machines were so extremely basic
It was a wonder they ever got off the ground
But true grit and determination won the day
And gradually progress in flight was found

Eventually the Royal Air Force was formed
To become our heritage since those early days
And they helped win our freedom in World War II
With courageous "dog-fights" that would amaze

Today we have such fantastic modern aircraft
That can be used in so many ways it is true
For defence or rescue, whatever the challenge
The Royal Air Force will always come through

It is also possible to select a destination
And travel to any country in the world
Where those massive jumbo jets can fly us
And so many enjoyable holidays are unfurled

Not forgetting the magnificent Red Arrows
Whose artistic aerobatics in the air
Make breath taking manoeuvres at great speed
Giving us all so much pleasure to share

They are usually chosen for the Grand Finale
Showing such clever flying skills for all to see
Which gives the Festival such a spectacular finish
And all proceeds go to the RAF charity

So our leader has arranged a second Concert
With some special songs you all know
To remember those very gallant airmen
Who fought many battles so long ago

Singing always gives us such pleasure
It helps lift our spirits off the ground
And as that very wise old saying goes
Music makes the world go round

Old-time Music Hall

The old-time music halls of days gone by
Are now far back in the past
But their wonderful songs will carry on
And their legacy will always last

Those clever artists who found such fame
Gave so much laughter and pleasure
To packed audiences every night
Who wanted to enjoy their leisure

I have tried to think of some famous names
Such as Marie Lloyd and Max Wall
But I know there are many others to find
Although my memory just can't recall

Those wonderful shows of yesteryear
Will never fade from view
No matter how long ago it was
The music always sounds like new

So have a good time this evening
And raise up your glasses one and all
To those artistic folk who did their best
And gave us the Old-time music hall

End of the tunnel

Even though things may look very black at present
And everything seems to be up against you
Remember there is always a light at the end of the tunnel
Where you will find lovely sunshine and skies of blue

It may be a very long battle as days pass by all too slowly
And these things do take a long time to repair
Remember there is always hope at the end of the tunnel
Where you will find fulfilment and satisfaction there

So take heart as you fight off this dark foe
And be strong for your caring family
Remember there is always love at the end of the tunnel
Where you will find contentment and joy for free

Winter

The Seasons

Winter brings along the cold dark gloomy days
But when snow falls it sparkles like jewels in the sun
Then Spring follows on with new life bursting all around
With snowdrops, primroses and daffodils showing Winter is done

Gradually glorious Summer follows with lovely warm weather
So many beautiful parks and woodland walks for all to enjoy
Delightful holidays on sandy beaches and exploring rocky pools
Endless time to spare to completely and thoroughly employ

Slowly the season changes into the rich colours of Autumn
Such awesome sights of the leaves turning red and gold
Another fabulous sight to observe in the countryside
As the days grow shorter and weather starts turning cold

...Then the circle of life is back to start another year

Winter Wishes

We are sending these Winter Wishes
With fondest love and good cheer
Hope you and your family enjoy
All the festivities at this time of year

Whilst sending these Winter Wishes
A very special one comes to mind
If only it could possibly come true
Then our lost happiness we should find

As we send all these Winter Wishes
It is hoped they will give to you
Good health, good luck and lots of joy
For Christmastime and all year through

If only…

Lost Cousin

A precious light has gone out in this world
And my dear Cousin will be so sadly missed by all
Fun loving, kind and full of character
She lived her long life to the full

Lots of chatter and infectious laughter
Will be her everlasting legacy
With happy memories of childhood days
And those special years with her wonderful family

Now there will be a new bright glittering star
Shining down from the heavens above
So that my dear Cousin will always be remembered
With such great affection and everlasting love

Family Thoughts

As Christmastime comes around again
My thoughts go back over many happy years
When we celebrated this special time together
With so much joy and laughter without any cares

We all looked forward to those wonderful days
And those surprise gifts from under the tree
Then enjoying a delicious Christmas meal together
We were such a loving and caring family

Now my thoughts bring back those great times
As they were always such pleasurable holidays
And I still think of all the fun we shared together
Which has given me such lovely memories always

Photo Shoot

After two happy years our Churchill Choir is still going strong
Now on a CD we have recorded a very catchy Christmas song
Words and music brilliantly composed called "Ring the Bells"
Which is mainly for a worthwhile charity, so we do hope it sells

Generously sponsored by Churchill, who had a two-day plan
To make a video film to launch our song, if we possibly can
So on day one we were taken to a special hotel so grand
Where they showed us how to use the video cameras by hand

The film crew then came with us in our groups of threes and fours
And helped us take Christmas scenes of Bournemouth outdoors
We walked all around the area, taking a lot of pretty views
And when lunch time was announced, it was indeed welcome news

After a very enjoyable lunch, we continued with our quest
And had a group session on a windy beach and pier, doing our best
But despite the cold wind and drizzle of rain, with thick raincoats on
We ended a very interesting day with a jolly group sing-a-long

On day two they took us to Southbourne All Saints Church hall
Where we were filmed decorating a Christmas tree that was quite tall
It was an extremely interesting day of Lights--Camera--Action
And was exciting to be part of such a lot of professional commotion

The film crew certainly worked very hard all through the day
Also providing delicious refreshments and hot drinks on a tray
We ended the afternoon session by singing our Christmas song
With the choir leader playing the piano well for so long

Our thanks to Churchill and the film crew who came
For giving us two days of enjoyment and a taste of fame
We send our best wishes and do hope it turns out to be
The best video film made to launch our Christmas CD

Thank You

Thanks for coming over the other day
It was so nice to see you all there
And it felt so good to be together again
To catch up with the family news we share

Such a joy to have lunch with you all
And to know that you are still doing fine
Despite all the many problems to be overcome
That fate keeps on dealing you all the time

As the years keep passing by so quickly
These meetings become more precious and dear
So thanks for all your kindness and fun
Have a good Christmas and a happy New Year

Winter's Christmas

Magical time of Year

It's Christmastime once again
That magical time of the year
When families all get together
To enjoy some festive good cheer

But this year it won't be the same
As there will be an empty chair
And no words can ever express
The deep sadness that we all share

But without all your loving kindness
We just couldn't have coped, it's true
Our most grateful thanks for everything
You really did help us get through

We both send you our very best wishes
With all our fondest love, dear
Good health and every happiness
For Christmas and the New Year

Special Time

It has been another long year
As Christmas comes again
With plenty of ups and downs
And lots of anguish, illness and pain

But as we try to celebrate
This special time of year
We have such precious memories
Of our two children so dear

We had a wonderful family
And we cherished all those happy years
When we shared our lives together
But sadly it all ended with so many tears

Now as we both keep plodding on
Along our very shaky path
I send you dear husband all my fondest love
Hoping we can still enjoy a good laugh

Just us two

Christmas comes around once again
It is that magical time of year
With all the pretty festive decorations
But now there is just the two of us dear

It has been a very difficult time for us both
When we lost Dad, it has not been the same
But things are gradually coming under control
With such an exciting new outlook to gain

Thanks so much for all your hard work
And for all your loving kindness and care
Just don't know how I would have coped
If my darling "Wheely" had not been there

We always did make a jolly good team
Through all the good times and some bad
Now I wish you lots of happiness and joy
For the best daughter a Mum ever had

Christmastime

A little robin in the snow
Bunches of holly and mistletoe
Pretty lights and tinsel on the tree
It's Christmastime for all to see

Lovely carols being sung
Special stockings being hung
Bringing back sweet memories
It's Christmastime for you and me

Turkey and all its trimmings to eat
Minces pies and pudding always a treat
Exciting parcels that give such joy
It's Christmastime for every girl and boy

Now in the warmth of the firelight glow
We think of our loved ones lost long ago
Such a bitter-sweet time to reminisce
It's Christmastime and a Christmas wish

Christmas Bells

The Christmas bells are ringing
Lovely carols being sung
It's that special time of year
When friends and family have fun

Pretty lights are glittering
Preparations have begun
Lots of exciting parcels
Waiting to be undone

A candle in the window
The holly and mistletoe being hung
Remembering lost loved ones
Now this Special Day has come

Christmas Sharing

It is that special time of year again
When families get together to share
All the great excitement and happiness
And to show just how much they care

It has been another very good year for me
Thanks so much for all your help and advice
And for making my life so blissfully content
Because moving here has been so nice

Just don't know how I would have coped
Without my dear daughter to turn to
You are so very kind and considerate
Such a very special daughter in all you do

So all my good wishes and lots of joy
For another wonderful Christmas my dear
Hoping you have the best one yet
Followed by a very Happy New Year

Christmas Festivities

Those gorgeous rich colours of autumn
Have now faded into cold dark winter days
But the Christmas festivities are on the horizon
Heralding much cheer in so many ways

There is always a great deal of planning to do
To get it right for all the special celebrations
Christmas cards to send to family and friends
And lots to arrange with all the splendid decorations

A Christmas tree with baubles and twinkling lights
Exciting gifts in pretty paper to put under the tree
Then off out to gather some holly and mistletoe
To make some charming garlands for all to see

There will be many excited little children
All waiting and hoping that Santa will call
Then the thrill of opening their presents
On that very magical day of all

Church bells will be ringing loud and clear
With Christmas carols being sung all over the land
Folk will be celebrating in their own way
And many choirs will be performing so grand

We do hope you enjoy our last Christmas concert
Which will be our "swan-song" to end this festive season
As our friends need more time to spend with their family
So the Choir is being disbanded for that very good reason

It has been such a wonderful experience
Since our Churchill Choir was first begun
Way back in 2016 with our leader in charge
And her husband there with his clever wit and fun

We have all enjoyed our singing over the years
And we had so much fun making a Christmas CD
When she composed a very successful catchy little tune
Which made a great deal of cash for the Cancer charity

We shall certainly miss our weekly meetings
Especially all the happiness and laughter we shared
As we have all become such good friends together
And the boost in morale each week could not be compared

We should also like to sincerely thank you all
For supporting us right from the start
We have thoroughly enjoyed entertaining you
But now, sadly, the time has come for us to part

We do hope you enjoy all the Christmas festivities
With all the family and friends you hold dear
Have a really good time over the holidays
And our very best wishes for a Happy New Year

Sights and Sounds of Christmas

Those blazing hot days of summer are gone
And the colourful Autumn has passed in a trice
Now the long dark winter months are on their way
Usually quite chilly with maybe some snow and ice

But the familiar sights and sounds of Christmas
Will most certainly help to lift the gloom
As everyone begins to plan and prepare
For that very special big day coming soon

There are so many really lovely traditions
That can be seen and heard everywhere
But despite all the extra hard work involved
It is nice to invite family and friends over to share

It has become such a very iconic time of year
With a great deal of things all going on
Parties being organised to have a good time
And everyone hoping that nothing goes wrong

Delicious meals to be cooked to perfection
Tasty sausage rolls and mince pies to eat
Plenty of good food and wine to tempt us all
So many wonderful choices are quite a treat

Such a very hectic season for all concerned
With Christmas cards to write and gifts to wrap
There never seems enough time to get it all done
As we try hard not to get into a last minute flap

Christmas trees waiting to be splendidly adorned
With coloured baubles and tinsel sparkling in the light
Exciting parcels placed carefully under the tree
And a shining white star on top to complete the sight

Pretty decorations to put up around our homes
Including symbolic bunches of holly and mistletoe
Children's festive stockings waiting to be filled
Such excitement and anticipation that we all know

The streets all lit up with their dazzling displays
Giving the busy people passing by a lot of joy
With the shops following suit with magical lights
A visit to Santa's grotto for every girl and boy

School children performing their nativity plays
With their childish skills and genuine ability
Giving pleasure to one and all who are there
It is another very traditional sight to go and see

It is so moving to hear the beautiful choirs singing
And see all the candles with their lovely warm glow
In honour of our Lord's birthday celebration
The church bells ring out the message we all know

There are so many traditional sights and sounds
To see and hear at this magical time of year
They all contribute towards making it so memorable
And giving everyone much happiness and good cheer

Christmas Memories

Christmas comes but once a year
And when it comes there is good cheer
But sometimes it brings a little tear
For our loved ones who can't be here

A little robin in the snow
Christmas lights all aglow
Pretty parcels tied with a bow
Giving joy to all we know

Lovely carols being sung
Christmas bells all being rung
Such a special time for everyone
With joy and happiness never done

Many Christmastimes have now gone
But still we have to keep plodding on
Doing our best when all is said and done
To remember Christmastimes with our dear son

It's a Joyful Christmastime

There are so many things we all hold dear
Especially at this lovely time of year
Giving us much happiness and good cheer
It's a joyful Christmastime

Bunches of holly and mistletoe
Christmas lights all aglow
A little robin in the snow
It's a joyful Christmastime

Lots of pretty parcels under the tree
Children's excitement wanting to see
Enjoying their parties with such glee
It's a joyful Christmastime

Getting together as families do
Remembering lost loved ones we once knew
Giving and sharing making dreams come true
It's a joyful Christmastime

Church bells ringing out across the land
Carols being sung by choirs so grand
Everyone celebrating hand in hand
It's a joyful Christmastime

All the heavenly hosts singing hallelujah
The Lord has come to be our Saviour
Be kind to each other and your neighbour
It's a joyful Christmastime

It all began one cold winter's night
When shepherds suddenly saw a very bright light
Which gave them all such a big fright
It's a joyful Christmastime

Then three wise men travelling from afar
Were loyally following that beautiful star
Until they saw the stable with its door ajar
It's a joyful Christmastime

Such a wonderful story for all to remember
Told with great reverence every December
When the Holy child was born and laid in a manger
It's a joyful Christmastime

That miraculous event came to show us the way
And to give us all hope each and every day
As love is always there come what may
Behold – it's a most joyful Christmastime

Good Wishes

It has certainly proved to be a most difficult year
For you and all your loving family who are so dear
But your strong will and courage has helped you through
Let's hope it will be a much better New Year for all of you

I do look forward very much to our weekly chats
It is so nice to catch up on family news and facts
Always good to know some are keeping well as it stands
While others are being looked after and in good hands

Do hope all the fun and laughter never ends
As you share it all with your family and friends
So relax and have a really wonderful time
You deserve to be pampered with good food and wine

Happy New Year

Christmastime is now over
The festivities are all done
Another year has just started
Bringing new hope to everyone

Perhaps it will be a new beginning
To help us through our sorrows
And give us the courage we need
To face some difficult tomorrows

So with lots of good wishes in mind
We do hope this will be a good year
And be full of good health and happiness
With plenty of joy and good cheer

Winter's New Hope

The strange year of 2020 has changed our lives so completely
When a deadly virus suddenly came and caused such fear
So far it has taken many precious lives without exception
Of those very special family members that we loved so dear

Such an extremely terrible situation has come to pass
And every country has been affected world-wide
Because when this unknown very dangerous foe strikes
It swallows all mankind like an incoming tide

So a complete lockdown of the country was put in place
As quickly as it was possible to achieve
To hold back the infection rate as much as possible
And our hope is to make this shocking virus finally leave

Every day our scientists struggle to find a cure
Such a big task for them all but they have to try
Which in these very dark times gives us a glimmer of hope
With a light at the end of a dark tunnel to keep spirits high

Now at last the lockdown is gradually easing
And cautiously we begin to start again
There is so much disruption to try and put right
After such a great deal of tragedy and pain

But the sky is still blue and the birds are full of song
Giving us a very good reason to do our best to cope
And so we will continue to battle against this alien virus
With overwhelming courage and a great deal of hope

... so here's to our future ...

The Challenge Fulfilled

… It has been quite a big undertaking
Compiling all my poems for final selection
But now at last all the hard work is over
Now waiting for acceptance of my collection

I have thoroughly enjoyed all the hard work involved
Going over my poems of the years now past
And to eventually have my poems in print
In a special edition of my Winter Tales book at last

Printed in Great Britain
by Amazon

52032403R00066